ROAD TO RESILIENCE

Life Lessons Learned Navigating Success in Auto Transport

Keith Jones

An imprint of Consultor Plus Auto

Copyright © 2026 by Keith Jones. All rights reserved.

No part of this book may be reproduced, stored in a retrieval system, or transmitted in any form or by any means, electronic, mechanical, photocopying, recording, or otherwise, without the express written permission of the publisher.

ISBN: 979-8-9951726-0-4 (paperback)

ISBN: 979-8-9951726-1-1 (ebook)

Library of Congress Control Number: 2026905992

Cover design by Nicole M. Palmer

Edited by Nicole Palmer of Nicole Williams Collective

Printed in the United States of America

Dedication

This book is dedicated...

To my wife, the mother of our three beautiful daughters — this journey has been ours. Every lesson, every late-night conversation, every moment of doubt followed by renewed faith... You were there. Thank you for walking beside me, believing in me, and holding the vision even when it felt distant. And for being right more times than I've been willing to admit out loud.

To my daughters, thank you for understanding when I missed games, activities, and family time. Even when I wasn't physically present, I was always with you in spirit. You are my reason and my motivation. Every mile was for you.

To the universal principles and divine practices that have shaped and guided me, making it possible to go from just imagining this journey to becoming an author. Without my faith in God, I am nothing. With it, I have learned I can become anything. For every time I thought I could do life on my own, God reminded me that we are meant to walk this path with those He places in our lives — for a purpose far greater than ourselves.

THE ROAD TO RESILIENCE

Table of Contents

Acknowledgments

I want to thank my mother, my late stepdad, and my late grandparents – whose strength, prayers, and presence shaped me into a man who doesn't give up. You never told me I couldn't do something, even when my ideas sounded far-fetched. If you couldn't see the vision, you still gave me space to build it. That kind of love is rare, and I honor it.

To my siblings – thank you for trusting my leadership and for giving me the grace to grow as I navigate life's complexities.

To my brothers from another mother – you inspire me every day. Thank you for being proof that iron sharpens iron. Our resilience has always been a shared language, and it continues to push me forward.

To my family in Northeast Baltimore – you will always be home. I carry you with me everywhere I go. I hope my journey shows that you don't have to surrender to circumstances or accept society's limitations to rise and succeed.

To everyone who contributed to this journey in any capacity — thank you. Each word of support, every act of aid, and every moment of trust made a difference.

And to my wife and children — every early morning, late night, and mile traveled... I can't fully fathom the emotional weight you carried, knowing each trip involved sacrifice and real danger. Thank you for loving me through all seasons, efforts, and changes.

The role of a driver was just one stop along the way — a chapter that taught me more about myself and the world so that we could rise higher together. This book is proof that our story matters. Every storm we weathered was preparation. Our love, our struggles, our faith, our growth — they've shaped us into who we were always meant to be.

Our journey didn't start with trucking – it started with purpose, love, and a divine mission to nurture what God placed inside us. This is only the beginning. The best is yet to come.

Special thanks to Nicole Palmer for helping me clarify my ideas and find my voice to write this book.

A Letter to Aspiring Auto Transporters

Dear Aspiring Auto Transporter,

If you're reading this, you're standing at the edge of something real. Maybe you're excited. Maybe you're a little scared. Both are the right responses. I've been exactly where you are — curious about this industry, unsure of what it truly demands, and hungry for a path that could change my family's story.

I'm writing to you not just as someone who made it work, but as someone who failed, got stranded, missed birthdays, and still chose to keep going. There was a moment — and I'll tell you the full story in this book — when I flew alone to Salt

Lake City to pick up a semi-truck I'd never driven, in a city I didn't know, with nothing but a one-way ticket and a whole lot of nerves. I stood next to that truck and genuinely thought about turning around, going back to the airport, and flying home to Atlanta. Fear had a grip on me that day. But I climbed in anyway. And that three-and-a-half-day drive back to Atlanta, heart racing the entire way, became one of the most defining experiences of my life.

That's what this letter is about. Not just the mechanics of auto transport — though we'll cover those too. It's about what happens inside of you when you commit to something bigger than your comfort zone.

The transportation industry is where every mile is more than just distance covered. It's a journey toward mastering a craft that goes beyond moving vehicles from point A to point B. It's about understanding the heartbeat of commerce, the trust your clients place in you, and the weight of delivering something that matters to someone else.

As a transporter, you're not just moving goods. You're moving someone's livelihood — their aspirations, their hard work, sometimes their dreams. Handle it with care and intention. That philosophy has guided everything I've built.

Embrace the learning curve. Auto transporting is more than driving. It's logistics, customer service, time management, equipment knowledge, and daily problem-solving. Each day brings new challenges and new chances to grow. Don't be too proud to ask questions or lean on experienced peers. This industry thrives on shared knowledge and genuine camaraderie.

Invest in your relationships. Whether with clients, fellow transporters, or brokers, these connections will become the bedrock of your business. Networking isn't just about expanding your client base. It's about building a support system that can guide you through the moments when the road gets hard.

Let technology be your ally. From GPS tracking to load boards and fleet management tools, the right technology streamlines operations and keeps you competitive. Stay current, and stay adaptable.

And please — do not underestimate self-care. Long hours on the road take a toll on your body and your mind. Prioritize rest. Eat well. Stay active. For me, audio podcasts became a lifeline on long drives — a way to turn windshield time into learning time. A healthy, growing transporter is a safe and effective one.

Most importantly, believe in yourself. There will be triumphs, and there will be setbacks. Both will shape you. The road may be long and the loads heavy, but I promise you — the journey is worth every mile.

Here's to safe travels, successful deliveries, and a career that means something.

Sincerely,

Keith Jones

Husband. Father. Entrepreneur. Seasoned Auto Transporter.

INTRODUCTION

The Dynamic World of Auto Transport

Welcome to the dynamic, ever-changing world of auto transport — a realm where the rubber meets the road and every journey weaves a unique story into the broader fabric of commerce and human connection. In this world, vehicles are more than metal and machinery. They're the backbone of an industry that bridges gaps, connects people, and fuels economies.

This book isn't just a guide. It's the story of a journey I've lived mile by mile — from the streets of Baltimore to the open highways of this country, from a man trying to survive to a business owner building something that lasts. The life of an auto transporter demands resilience, adaptability, and an unshakeable commitment to doing the job right.

Whether you're an experienced transporter, brand new to the industry, or simply curious about how this world works, there's something in these pages for you. We'll explore the art and science of moving vehicles safely and efficiently, the logistical challenges, the personal sacrifices, and the unexpected rewards.

This is a profession where each day brings a new puzzle. Weather, traffic, mechanical failures, paperwork, difficult clients — they're all part of the landscape. But so are the open road, the freedom, the financial opportunity, and the pride of delivering something that matters to someone.

Beyond the logistics, this business is about people. The clients who trust you with their property. The fellow transporters who share the road and the struggle. The family waiting at home. Strong relationships are what make or break a long career in this industry.

The auto transport world is also constantly evolving — driven by technology, market forces, and a changing global economy. Staying competitive means being willing to learn, adapt, and grow alongside the industry.

So buckle up. The journey ahead is enlightening, honest, and full of hard-won wisdom. Let's hit the road.

CHAPTER 1

The Foundational Skills and Experience

Learning the Craft Before You Drive the Load

My journey into auto transport began not with a truck, but with a mindset shift. I came to understand quickly that this industry is far more intricate than it appears from the outside. It's not simply about moving vehicles from one location to another. It's a carefully orchestrated effort that requires skill, precision, and a deep respect for the responsibility you carry.

Think of it like an orchestra. Every section has a role. Every instrument matters. I've had the privilege of playing a crucial part in that coordination, and it's shaped everything about how I approach this work.

The Day It Became Real: Salt Lake City

Before I talk about skills and systems, I want to tell you about the moment this industry stopped being theoretical for me.

I had to fly to Salt Lake City, Utah, to pick up a semi-truck. Alone. No co-driver. No one who'd done it before standing next to me. Just me, a plane ticket, and the assumption that I'd figure it out.

I landed, got to the truck, and stood there looking at it. And I'll be honest with you — I had several very serious thoughts about leaving that truck right where it was, walking back into the airport, and flying home to Atlanta. Not because I couldn't drive. But because everything about that moment was unknown. The truck. The route. The terrain. The distance. The weight of it all — literally and figuratively.

Fear is a strange thing. It doesn't always show up as hesitation. Sometimes it shows up as perfectly reasonable logic. My brain was giving me every sensible argument for why I should turn around. And for a few minutes, I genuinely entertained it.

But I climbed in.

The drive from Salt Lake City back to Atlanta took about three and a half days. My heart was racing for most of it. Every merge, every mountain pass, every moment of unfamiliar terrain required me to dig into reserves I didn't know I had. I stopped when I needed to. I called when I needed to. I prayed more than a few times.

And I made it.

That drive didn't just deliver a truck. It delivered something in me. It proved that the gap between fear and capability is often smaller than we think — and that the only way to close it is to move forward anyway. Everything I've learned about this industry since then has been built on that foundation: the willingness to do the hard thing when every instinct is telling you to stop.

I tell this story because if you're new to this work, your Salt Lake City moment is coming. It might be your first time loading a car hauler alone. Your first long-haul run in bad weather. Your first difficult client. Whatever it is — the fear is normal. What you do with it is what defines your career.

Understanding the Industry Landscape

The auto transport industry is more diverse than most people realize. Open carriers — the dependable workhorses — provide an affordable and widely used method for transporting vehicles. Enclosed carriers offer heightened protection for luxury, classic, and high-value cars. Specialized transporters handle oversized or unusual vehicles that require custom solutions.

Beyond the equipment, success in this field demands a working knowledge of the legal and regulatory landscape — particularly Department of Transportation (DOT) regulations — along with the business fundamentals: networking, contract negotiation, logistics management, and detailed documentation. Underestimate any of these and you'll feel it on the road.

Mastering the Craft: Skills That Set You Apart

Driving proficiency in auto transport is an art form. It takes time, repetition, and genuine attention to detail to master maneuvering different types of transport vehicles through varied road conditions. Loading and unloading — particularly with high-value or non-operational vehicles — require precision that you can only develop through hands-on experience.

Mechanical knowledge is not optional in this business. It's a necessity. Understanding how your equipment works helps prevent breakdowns, reduces downtime, and keeps your operation running smoothly when others are stuck on the shoulder.

Here are the skills that have mattered most in my career:

- Exceptional customer service — building lasting relationships through clear communication, accountability, and a solutions-first mindset.
- Effective time management — understanding the rhythm of operations and knowing how to maximize every hour.
- Adaptability and problem-solving — because the unexpected is not a question of if, but when.

The Road to Mastery: How Experience Is Built

Experience in auto transport doesn't come from a textbook — it comes from the road. Every mile I've traveled has added to my understanding of this work. I started small, took on simpler loads, made mistakes, and learned from each one.

Seeking mentorship from experienced professionals made an enormous difference. Their wisdom saved me time, money, and a great deal of unnecessary pain. I also learned to document my journeys — to treat each run like a performance worth reviewing and improving.

Building a strong network of fellow transporters, industry contacts, and clients became the backbone of my business. That network acts as the backstage crew — offering support, advice, and collaborative opportunities when you need them most.

Daily Operations: The Foundation of Good Habits

Behind every successful transport is a set of consistent habits. The following checklists represent the baseline of professional operation. Master these, and you'll set yourself apart from the very beginning.

Pre-Trip Inspection

- Tires — Check pressure, tread wear, and secure attachment.

- Lights – Confirm headlights, taillights, turn signals, and brake lights are all functioning.
- Fluid Levels – Inspect engine oil, coolant, transmission fluid, and windshield washer fluid.
- Brakes – Test for responsiveness and proper function.
- Trailer Hitch – Confirm the hitch is secure and correctly connected to the towing vehicle.
- Safety Equipment – Verify reflective triangles, fire extinguisher, and first aid kit are present.
- Trailer Condition – Examine for any damage or wear that could impact safety.
- Load Securement – Ensure vehicles are properly secured with appropriate tie-downs, wheel straps, or chains.

En-Route Inspection

- Tire Pressure – Monitor during rest stops.
- Load Securement – Verify tie-downs and straps remain tight.
- Trailer Temperature – Monitor if transporting temperature-sensitive vehicles.

Post-Trip Inspection

- Exterior Inspection – Check trailer and towing vehicle for any new damage.

- Tire Inspection — Assess condition and adjust pressure as needed.
- Cleanliness — Wash the trailer and clear debris.
- Unload Vehicles — Execute a careful, damage-free unloading process.
- Documentation — Record any new damages or issues observed.

These inspections form the foundation of good habits in auto transport. One of the most important lessons I've taken from this work is this: the journey isn't just about transporting cars. It's about protecting something that matters to someone else — their dreams, their livelihood, sometimes the means to a better life. Honor that weight every time you hit the road.

KEY LESSONS FROM THIS CHAPTER

- *Fear is not a stop sign. It's a signal that what you're about to do actually matters. Do it anyway.*

- *Mastery in this industry is built mile by mile, not in a classroom.*
- *The checklist is not a formality. It is your first line of defense.*
- *Every transporter you respect started somewhere uncomfortable. That's where you are right now.*

CHAPTER 2

The Success Formula

Balance, Strategy, and the People Who Keep You Going

I remember buying my first trailer. The sleepless nights learning how to operate it. The long drives that tested my patience and endurance. There were breakdowns in the middle of nowhere, moments of serious doubt, and late nights when I quietly wondered whether I'd made the right call.

But through every challenge, I learned something deeper about myself: resilience isn't about never falling. It's about learning to get up stronger each time. The open road became my office, my sanctuary, and sometimes, my test. It constantly reminded me that true success means finding balance — not just fulfilling the demands of the job, but also showing up for the people who matter most.

As an auto transporter, a husband, and a father of three daughters, I've learned that the road to success isn't just paved with hard work — it's built on intention.

Structure as a Foundation

Early on, I learned the power of routine. Setting specific times for driving, administrative tasks, rest, and reflection wasn't optional — it was survival. Regular check-ins with my family, even a quick call or text while at a truck stop, helped bridge the distance my work sometimes created.

Maintaining physical and mental health became non-negotiable. Quick workouts, healthy meals, and moments of quiet reflection helped me stay sharp, grounded, and prepared for whatever lay ahead. The cab of a truck is a small space — but it can be a space of discipline and focus if you treat it that way.

The Financial Lesson Nobody Told Me About

Let me share something that took us longer than it should have to figure out, and I'm sharing it because I want to save you the headache.

In the early days, we made the mistake of spending our profits too quickly. The money would hit the account, and we'd feel like we were doing well. Bills are paid, family is fed, business is growing — let's celebrate. The problem is that in auto transport, the expenses that really matter — fuel, insurance, maintenance, repairs, registration — don't always line up with your deposits. Variable expenses have their own schedule.

So we learned, the hard way, to spend on the net, not the gross.

That distinction changed how we ran everything. The gross number is what you earn. The net number is what's actually yours after the business has taken its share for costs, taxes, and reserves. We started delaying our recreational spending. Not punishing ourselves, but building in a pause — a habit of waiting until the dust settled before deciding what was left to enjoy.

It sounds simple. And it is simple. But simple doesn't mean easy, especially when you've been grinding, and the money finally starts coming in. The temptation to reward yourself is real. The discipline to wait is what separates operators who build something lasting from those who stay stuck in the cycle of earning and scrambling.

Now I tell every new owner-operator I talk to: know the difference between what you made and what you kept. Build your lifestyle around the second number, not the first.

Strategies for Long-Term Success

Long-term success in this business isn't just about getting from point A to point B. It's about the journey, the discipline, and the people who ride along with you. My wife and children have been my anchors when the loads got heavy and the nights grew long.

From day one, I viewed my role not just as a job but as a business. I set long-term goals – expanding into a fleet, developing niche services, and creating new income streams within the industry. I learned to budget carefully, from fuel and maintenance to insurance and emergency reserves. That financial discipline is what allowed me to navigate the unpredictability of the road with confidence.

Education has been another pillar of longevity. I make it a priority to keep learning through networking, attending industry conferences, and staying connected with peers. The relationships I've built in those spaces have opened doors, offered insights, and shaped both my business and my character.

Case Studies: What Success Can Look Like

Here are a few real-world profiles of auto transporters who've carved their own paths — each offering a different model of what's possible.

The Adaptive Entrepreneur

Flexible and customer-oriented, this transporter starts with a small setup but quickly identifies the value in diversifying. They expand into transporting specialized vehicles such as boats and RVs — a profitable market that their competitors often overlook. The lesson: be willing to go where others won't.

The Tech-Savvy Transporter

Their background in technology transforms their operation. GPS tracking for the fleet, online booking systems for clients, data analytics to optimize routes and fuel efficiency — all of it reduces costs and increases competitive advantage. The lesson: innovation is not a luxury; it's a differentiator.

The Community Builder

They recognize the power of community early in their career. By building a network of fellow transporters — sharing leads, tips, and resources — they become a respected leader in the industry. The lesson: success in this business rarely happens in isolation.

Building a Resilient Business Model

Resilience comes from a combination of passion, planning, and adaptability. For me, it also meant diversifying income. Adding brokerage services alongside transportation was a strategic move to provide more value to clients and establish a more stable financial foundation.

Understanding the market is critical. Knowing when to take calculated risks and when to exercise caution has been central to my strategy. I've also learned to see mistakes not as failures but as tuition — paying for knowledge I couldn't get any other way.

Personal Growth and Professional Development

Throughout this journey, personal growth and professional development have been inseparable. Investing in myself through reading, mentorship, and workshops has consistently paid dividends in my business. Balancing work with family — being truly present when I'm home, making the most of that time — has always been a top priority.

The key to success in auto transport is not a single thing. It's a combination: hard work, strategic thinking, financial discipline, and a commitment to continuous improvement. Keep your hands steady on the wheel, your eyes on the horizon, and move forward with purpose.

---

8 Reliable Customer Bases for Auto Transporters

Building a steady customer base is one of the most important things you can do for the longevity of your business. Here are eight categories worth targeting — and how to approach each effectively.

1. Auto Auctions

Auctions are often the largest single source of vehicle transportation. Many have their own load boards or work with proprietary brokers. Get to know the auction staff, ask the right questions, and understand their expectations for inbound and outbound loads.

2. Auto Enthusiasts

Enthusiasts often know a wide network of people who need transport services. Find them through social media, auto shows, repair shops, and parts stores.

3. Car Clubs

Car clubs frequently travel state to state to showcase vehicles and are open to arranging loads directly. Search online for car show meetups, call local convention centers, and tap into Facebook groups to find active clubs.

4. Independent Dealers

Independent dealers are a strong and often overlooked revenue source. They pay upon delivery, allow for close working relationships, and sometimes buy additional vehicles to fill your trailer. Franchise dealers offer additional opportunities through used car delivery and trade-in transport.

5. Online Social Networking

Posting content about your daily life as a transporter – including live videos showing the process – has consistently generated inbound inquiries and quote requests. Social media makes your business visible in a way that word-of-mouth alone can't replicate.

6. Realtors

Real estate agents regularly work with clients who are relocating and need vehicle transport. Build relationships with local realtors by attending their events, providing tailored marketing materials, and offering referral incentives.

7. Sports and Talent Agencies

Athletes and entertainers often need vehicle transport services, sometimes on short notice. Connect with local talent agencies, propose both case-by-case and retainer arrangements, and attend industry events where agents and clients gather.

8. Load Boards

Research reputable transport brokerages and vehicle load boards. Offer competitive rates, maintain consistent reliability, and use customer portals or mobile apps to make booking seamless. Load boards work best as a complement to – not a replacement for – direct client relationships.

Final tip: always keep an eye on your operating costs – fuel, insurance, maintenance, and overhead. This helps you price competitively while protecting your margins. And never forget: great service generates referrals, and referrals build legacies.

KEY LESSONS FROM THIS CHAPTER

- *Spend on your net, not your gross. Know the difference between what you made and what you kept.*
- *Delay recreational spending until your variable expenses have settled. Build in a pause.*
- *Long-term success requires more than hard work. It requires intention, planning, and discipline in the quiet moments.*
- *Your network is part of your infrastructure. Invest in it like any other asset.*

CHAPTER 3

Navigating Challenges

Breakdowns, Storms, and the Road Within

Life doesn't always give a warning before it shifts gears.

I learned that at 17, when a series of bad decisions landed me behind bars. My world shrank to walls and routine, but even in that confined space, I found something I hadn't expected: reflection, accountability, and the hard truth about the power of choice.

When I was released from Maryland correctional institution, my stepdad was waiting — not with judgment, but with purpose. He put me to work and told me, "If you're going to drive, drive with purpose." Those words stuck.

Years later, a single phone call changed everything. There had been an accident. When I arrived, everything slowed — the flashing lights, the yellow tape, the mangled car. I ran toward it, praying it wasn't him. But it was. He was airlifted to Johns Hopkins, and shortly after, he was gone.

Losing him felt like losing my compass. For months, I replayed that moment in my mind. But eventually, grief turned into drive. His lessons became my inheritance. I decided to carry forward what he started — not just the trade, but the way he lived: steady, giving, and accountable.

Roadside Breakdowns: Every Driver's Test

Every transporter knows that a breakdown is not a question of if — it's a question of when. I've had my share. Once, midway through a tight schedule, my truck broke down without warning — miles from the nearest town. Stranded on the shoulder,

I had to shift instantly from driver to problem-solver. That experience taught me one of the most valuable lessons in this business: preparation is everything.

But one experience stands above them all. And I'm going to tell it to you in full, because I want you to understand what I mean when I say that safety is not optional.

The Night the Highway Hit Back

I was tired. Not the regular kind of road-weary tired that a coffee and a stretch can fix — I mean the deep, bone-heavy fatigue that comes from pushing too long without rest. I knew I needed to stop. So I pulled over on the side of the highway and made a decision that probably saved my life: I climbed out of the driver's seat, moved to the passenger side, and lay down to take a nap.

What I didn't do was set out my safety triangles. I engaged the truck and trailer brakes. I had my hazard lights off. I told myself I'd just rest for a minute — I'd set up the triangles when I got back up. That was the mistake.

I was asleep when it happened. It felt like an earthquake. A violent, disorienting jolt that sent particles flying through the cab and left my whole world tilted. An 18-wheeler had sideswiped my truck at speed — and kept going. Didn't stop. Just kept moving down the highway like nothing had happened.

I tried to get out through the driver's door. I slipped. The steps were gone. The fuel tank had been sheared off. The door opened into nothing. I eventually got out through the other side, stood on the highway shoulder, and looked at what remained.

Two cars I had been transporting were totaled. My fuel tank was damaged. The truck had taken a serious hit. And by some combination of engineering and grace, I was standing there to tell the story.

I give a lot of credit to the truck's design. I've always preferred units built with solid metal framing all around — the kind of construction that takes a hit and holds. That night, it held.

I called my safety department. They told me to call 911, which I did. And then I stood on that shoulder, in the dark, thinking about the triangle I'd left folded up in the cab.

Fifteen minutes. That's how long I had been parked before the impact. Fifteen minutes was all the margin I had — and I spent it without my safety equipment deployed.

I'm not telling this story to scare you. I'm telling it because the checklist is not a technicality. The triangles are not optional. The hazard lights are not a suggestion. Every step of your safety protocol exists because someone, somewhere, learned the hard way. Sometimes that person was me.

Three Principles I Live By

1. Prevent Whenever Possible

Your truck and trailer are your lifelines. Treat them accordingly. Build a routine inspection checklist and follow it without exception. Pay attention to sights, sounds, and smells. These subtle cues often give you an early warning before something becomes a costly breakdown. Invest in quality parts and timely servicing — it will save you far more than it costs.

2. Adopt an Emergency Mindset

Despite your best prevention efforts, breakdowns will still happen. Keep a well-stocked emergency kit: basic tools, spare parts, flares, and reflective triangles. Know your insurance claim process in advance. Maintain accounts with nationwide fleet service centers along your regular routes. Having help lined up before you need it is not paranoia — it's professionalism.

3. Handle It with Safety First

When a breakdown or roadside stop occurs, your first priority is always safety. Move your vehicle to a safe position. Put on high-visibility gear. Deploy your warning triangles immediately — before you do anything else. Before you check your phone. Before you close your eyes. Triangles first.

Stay calm. Assess the situation clearly. Communicate with your clients, your dispatcher, and any relevant safety personnel. Transparency in a crisis builds the kind of trust that outlasts the problem.

Navigating Traffic and Weather

As a transporter, traffic and weather are constants you can't control but must always prepare for.

Traffic Navigation

Use real-time traffic apps and GPS systems with traffic analysis built in. Plan your routes around peak hours and known congestion points. Staying ahead of delays protects both your schedule and your client relationships.

Weathering the Storm

From scorching summer heat to winter ice storms, weather can shift fast and dramatically.

Adjust your driving style to match the conditions. Slow down in adverse weather, increase your following distance, and carry weather-appropriate gear. Stay informed through forecasts, and always be ready to change your route or pull off entirely if conditions become unsafe.

I remember a winter night when a sudden snowstorm struck unexpectedly. The roads were icy, visibility was near zero, and I was responsible for transporting valuable vehicles. My priority was clear: safety first, then communication. I slowed down, took necessary breaks, and kept every client informed about potential delays. What surprised me was the response — rather than frustration, I earned deeper loyalty. Customers value consistent, honest communication, especially when things don't go as planned.

Paperwork and Regulatory Compliance

Paperwork may not carry the drama of a highway breakdown, but it carries just as much consequence. From bills of lading to insurance documents, staying organized is non-negotiable.

Create a reliable system for managing your documents — both physical and digital. Use mobile apps to scan and track paperwork on the go. And when it comes to regulatory compliance, stay current. Hours of service rules, load limits, vehicle standards — know them. Consider joining industry associations or forums to stay informed and connected with other professionals.

The Psychological Side of the Road

The life of an auto transporter is not only a physical challenge — it's a mental and emotional marathon.

Long hours on the road can be lonely. Establish routines that keep you connected with the people who matter. Find ways to decompress during breaks — podcasts, audiobooks, music, or simply quiet reflection. Some of us genuinely thrive in solitude, using the road as a place to think clearly and find peace.

For me, one of the most valuable habits I've developed is using drive time for microlearning. I listen to audio podcasts while I'm behind the wheel — business, leadership, personal development, industry news. Hours that might otherwise feel like dead time become some of the most productive hours of my day. When I pull into a delivery, and someone asks what I've been thinking about, the answer is usually something I just learned in the cab.

The windshield can be a classroom. Let it be one.

Prioritize your physical and mental health without compromise. Simple exercises, a balanced diet, and adequate sleep are foundational. And don't hesitate to seek professional support if the weight of the road gets heavy. Your well-being is not just personal — it affects everyone who depends on you.

Balancing Business and Family

There were times when I missed important family milestones because of this job. Those moments clarified something important for me: maintaining a healthy work-life balance isn't just about scheduling. It's about being intentional. Setting aside specific times for family, even while traveling. Being fully present when you're home.

Financial Uncertainties

The auto transport industry has a rhythm of highs and lows that will test your financial discipline constantly. Managing cash flow during slow seasons requires foresight and planning. I learned to save aggressively during profitable months and spend carefully when business slowed.

Diversifying income streams — transport brokerage, vehicle sales, consulting — helped create stability when one revenue source dipped. And I make a point of sharing this reality with anyone considering the owner-operator path: the financial side of this business is just as important as the driving side.

Learning from Every Challenge

Each challenge has been a lesson, and each lesson has made me better. Recognizing that every breakdown builds resilience, every difficult load sharpens your problem-solving, and every mile of hard road deepens your experience — that perspective is what keeps you going.

Steps for Loading Vehicles Safely

1. Pre-Loading Inspection

- Conduct a thorough walk-around to check for pre-existing damage.
- Document the vehicle's condition with photos or video.
- Confirm the vehicle is in drivable condition with adequate fuel and operational brakes.

2. Preparing the Trailer

- Check the trailer for structural damage or issues.
- Ensure ramps and decks are clean, clear, and dry.
- Position ramps correctly and confirm they're securely attached.

3. Positioning the Vehicle

- Approach the ramp slowly and align the vehicle with the center.
- Use a spotter if available to guide even weight distribution.
- Mind the vehicle's clearance to avoid undercarriage damage.

4. Loading the Vehicle

- Drive or winch the vehicle onto the trailer carefully, at a steady pace.
- Avoid sudden movements or stops.
- Stop the vehicle at the predetermined position to maintain weight balance.

5. Securing the Vehicle

- Use wheel straps or tie-downs at each corner, attached to designated tie-down points.
- Tighten straps firmly to remove slack without over-tightening.
- Test by gently rocking the vehicle to confirm it's fully secured.

6. Safety Checks

- Walk the perimeter to inspect all tie-downs for proper tension.
- Confirm the parking brake is engaged and the transmission is in park or neutral.

- Check for any loose items that could become dislodged in transit.

7. Documenting Post-Loading Condition

- Record the vehicle's condition after loading and note any changes.
- Update transport documentation with observations from the loading process.

8. Final Trailer Inspection

- Verify all lights, reflectors, and signals are functioning.
- Confirm the trailer's weight is within legal limits and evenly distributed.
- Check hitch connections, safety chains, and brake lines one final time.

KEY LESSONS FROM THIS CHAPTER

- *Deploy your safety triangles before you do anything else on a roadside stop. Before your phone. Before your eyes close. Triangles first.*
- *Fatigue is a decision point. The professional choice is always to stop.*
- *Your windshield time is an opportunity. Use it to learn.*

- *Every breakdown is teaching you something. Stay curious enough to find out what.*

CHAPTER 4

From Setbacks to Milestones

How Hard Times Became Turning Points

Every setback I faced became a stepping stone. Every challenge shaped me into the entrepreneur, husband, and father I am today.

But to understand how far I've come, you have to understand where this business actually started – not in a boardroom, not with a business plan, and not with my idea.

It started with my wife being right.

Wifey Saw It First

When the pandemic hit in 2020, and car sales came to a near-complete halt, I was at a crossroads. The industry I'd been working in had gone quiet. The income had dried up. And the path forward wasn't clear.

My wife had been suggesting the auto transport route for a while. Not hinting at it — telling me. She could see the opportunity. She could see where our skills, our network, and our hustle could take us if we made the pivot. But I wasn't ready to hear it. I had my own ideas about what the next chapter should look like, and her idea wasn't in that picture yet.

Then the moment came when it became undeniable that she was right.

And I had to figure out how to go back to her and say that.

I'm being honest with you: that conversation wasn't easy for me. Not because she made it hard — but because admitting you were wrong to the person who told you so takes a specific kind of humility that doesn't always come naturally. She was gracious about it, but she was also very clear. She had seen it. She had waited. And now here we were.

We sold what we could. We bought a trailer. And we built our transport business from nothing but faith, grit, and two people who were fully committed to making it work.

The lesson I carry from that moment isn't just about business. It's about partnership. The person beside you often sees things about your life and your future that your own proximity won't allow you to see. Listen to them. Especially when it costs you some pride.

The First Load: A Revelation

Those early days were hard in ways I didn't expect. I hauled cars overnight, learned mechanical work through trial and error, and discovered that every breakdown was a classroom. My wife handled dispatching and paperwork while managing our home and our daughters. Together, we became a team.

But the first load changed something in me that I hadn't anticipated.

I went into it expecting it to feel like a grind — necessary, maybe, but exhausting. What I didn't expect was the revelation of what the Hours of Service regulations actually made possible. Under those rules, I could give 68 hours of service over a set period. And within that structure, I discovered I could generate the same income — sometimes more — than I had in previous work, with loads that were more readily available.

The math hit differently than I expected. The structure that I thought would limit me was actually protecting me. It was forcing the kind of discipline that makes a business sustainable instead of just intense.

Our daughters watched it all unfold. I made sure they understood why we were doing it. Not for comfort. For freedom. Because that's what this road truly represents — freedom earned mile by mile.

Georgia: The Move That Almost Made Us Quit

If the first load was a revelation, the move to Georgia was a reckoning.

When we relocated, our income appeared to drop. Not because the business was failing — but because the economy we moved into operates on a completely different scale than the one we came from. It was apples to oranges. Where we came from had a higher cost of living, higher rates, and a market that priced accordingly. Georgia's economy was lower cost of living, which meant lower rates and different expectations.

But when you're in the middle of it, it doesn't feel like an economic comparison. It feels like failure. It feels like you made the wrong move. It feels like maybe this whole thing isn't going to work.

We had that conversation. Seriously. We sat with the discomfort of wondering whether we'd made a mistake coming here.

What got us through it was two things: doing the actual math, and refusing to compare the new market to the old one on the old market's terms. Once we understood the economy we were operating in — what clients here expected, what rates were realistic, what volume was available — we could build a strategy for it instead of fighting against it.

The lesson: a reduction in income isn't always a business problem. Sometimes it's a context problem. Understand your market before you judge your results.

The Inevitability of Setbacks

No journey is without its hurdles. In auto transport, setbacks are not the exception — they are part of the business. The key is not to avoid them, because you can't. The key is to develop the resilience and resourcefulness to overcome them and keep moving.

Mechanical Failures

Engine breakdowns, transmission troubles, tire blowouts — these are common and often expensive. They don't just cause delays; they test your ability to stay calm and solve problems under pressure.

Market Fluctuations

Fuel price hikes, insurance rate increases, shifts in consumer behavior — the auto transport industry moves with economic tides. When the market shifts, your business has to shift with it.

Customer Service Challenges

Disputes over delivery timing, vehicle condition, or billing issues happen. What I've learned is this: reaching out proactively with updates — even when things don't go as planned — is what separates professionals from everyone else. Silence in a difficult situation is almost always the wrong choice.

Family: The Weight Behind the Wheel

One of the most significant personal challenges I've faced in this career has been finding harmony between a demanding profession and my family life. My wife has been a constant source of strength. My daughters have been my motivation.

But this work asks a price. Unpredictable schedules. Tight deadlines. And sometimes – missing moments I can never get back.

I want to be honest about that. Not to discourage you, but to prepare you. And to say this: when I was able to bring one of my daughters along for a day on the road, everything changed. Those hours gave her a real window into her dad's world. She saw what I do. She understood the precision, the patience, and the responsibility it takes. It gave us time together that most jobs simply can't offer.

Navigating the Financial Landscape

Managing finances in auto transport is like riding a rollercoaster. The discipline I've built around spending on the net rather than the gross has been central to our stability. During the profitable months, we saved. During the slow months, we were ready.

Diversifying income became essential: my wife launched a transport brokerage to handle assignments I couldn't take directly. We also bought and resold vehicles. Both created vertical growth and allowed our family business to breathe.

Transforming Setbacks into Wisdom

Every breakdown taught me more about my equipment. Every market shift taught me more about adaptability. Every difficult customer taught me something about communication and grace under pressure.

Resilience isn't something you're born with. It's built. Every setback you navigate adds another layer. Every challenge you overcome prepares you for a bigger one.

- Develop a problem-solving mindset. Train yourself to see obstacles as puzzles to solve, not walls to stop you.
- Build a support system. Peers, mentors, and industry contacts become your network of wisdom and encouragement.
- Embrace self-care. Rest, exercise, and nutrition are not luxuries for a transporter. They're operational requirements.
- Celebrate small victories. They are the fuel that keeps you moving forward.

KEY LESSONS FROM THIS CHAPTER

- *The person beside you often sees your future before you do. Listen to them — especially when it costs you some pride.*
- *A reduction in income isn't always a business problem. Sometimes it's a context problem. Understand your market.*
- *The structure of this industry — Hours of Service, regulations, systems — is not your enemy. It's your framework.*
- *Every setback is a hidden milestone. You won't always see it in the moment. Keep going anyway.*

CHAPTER 5

The Power of Delegation

You Can't Drive Every Lane at Once

Your business is like your child. You nurture it, protect it, and sometimes struggle to trust anyone else with it. But just like parenting, if you try to carry everything yourself, you'll eventually burn out — and neither you nor your business will be at its best.

Learning to ask for help and mastering the art of delegation have been among the most important and humbling lessons of my career. As a husband, father of three girls, and business owner, I've come to understand that delegation is not a sign of weakness. It's a sign of leadership. It's how you protect your time, your health, your family, and your vision.

The First Time I Tried to Delegate: A Lesson in Misalignment

I want to tell you how delegation actually started for me, because it didn't go the way I planned.

We were receiving more load dispatches than I could personally handle. The volume was higher than expected – a good problem to have, but a problem nonetheless. I needed help. So I enlisted a buddy. Someone I trusted. Someone I thought I knew well enough to bring into the work.

I started training him. Showed him the process, the standards, the expectations. And fairly quickly, I realized something uncomfortable: his work ethic did not align with mine. The way he approached the job – the attention to detail, the sense of urgency, the pride in doing it right –

wasn't what I needed. And the loads don't wait for someone to get comfortable.

I ended up finishing the work myself.

It was frustrating. But it was also clarifying. Because that experience answered a question I'd been sitting with: if I can't consistently find people whose standards match mine, how do I scale this thing?

That's when my wife and I started the brokerage. Not just as an income diversification strategy – though it became that too – but specifically to build a network of more qualified transporters we could confidently delegate work to. People who had already been vetted. People who had a track record. People whose standards we could verify before the load ever left the yard.

The failed delegation attempt didn't set us back. It built the foundation for something far more sustainable.

Why Delegation Matters in Auto Transport

In the fast-paced world of auto transport, where time is money and precision is everything, delegation isn't just a nice-to-have management skill – it's a survival strategy.

In the early days, I felt overwhelmed by the sheer volume of tasks required to run the business. Driving. Dispatching. Paperwork. Customer communication. Maintenance scheduling. Trying to do all of it myself meant doing none of it well. My skills and time were best spent on the road, building client relationships, and focusing on the core of the business. Everything else needed a home somewhere else.

Three Areas Where Delegation Changed Everything

1. Maximizing Time

By delegating administrative and routine tasks to capable hands, I was able to concentrate on what I do best: driving and building client trust. The time I reclaimed was time I could reinvest into the business and into my family.

2. Scaling Operations

Expansion was always the goal, but scaling without sacrificing quality felt like an impossible task when I was doing everything alone. Through strategic delegation, we were able to broaden our services, take on more clients, and diversify our portfolio – while maintaining the standards we'd built our reputation on.

3. Reducing Burnout

There were moments when the pressure of running every aspect of the business alone took a real toll on my well-being. Delegation didn't just redistribute the workload – it brought fresh energy, new ideas, and a renewed sense of possibility. A one-man show has limits. A team has potential.

Personal Reflections on Letting Go

The transition to effective delegation wasn't instant and it wasn't comfortable. It involved understanding the strengths of the people around me, communicating my expectations clearly, and building a foundation of trust. It required me to let go of my need to control every detail — and that, for someone who takes pride in precision, was a gradual process.

But the results have been deeply rewarding. Professionally, it empowered my team, fostered a collaborative culture, and pushed our business to new heights. Personally, it gave me back time with my family — time to be present for the moments that matter and can't be rescheduled.

Identifying What to Delegate

As we expanded from motor carrier operations into transport brokerage, we quickly recognized that handling everything alone was unsustainable. Here are the areas we found most critical to delegate:

- Administrative Tasks — Invoicing, scheduling, and client follow-up are time-intensive but not always the highest use of the operator's time.
- Maintenance and Repairs — Routine maintenance and repairs are critical to fleet performance. Knowing when to handle them yourself and when to trust a qualified mechanic is part of good business judgment.

We also learned to consult outside strategists — website developers, business coaches — people who could bring expertise we didn't have. Sometimes the best ideas are the ones you didn't come up with yourself.

Overcoming the Challenges of Delegation

- Finding Reliable Help — Use industry networks, ask for referrals, and conduct thorough interviews. Trust is earned, not assumed.
- Relinquishing Control — Delegating tasks does not mean losing control of your business. It means managing it more intelligently.

- Investing in Training – Time spent training your team pays dividends. Well-trained people require less supervision and produce better results.

Technology as a Delegation Tool

- Transport Management Systems (TMS) – We've used Super Dispatch since 2019. Automated scheduling, routing, and billing reduce manual work significantly.
- Communication Platforms – Tools like Slack or Microsoft Teams keep teams aligned and informed without requiring constant check-ins.
- Cloud-Based Documentation – Google Drive and Dropbox ensure that essential documents are accessible to the right people at the right time.

The Rewards of Effective Delegation

- Increased productivity – when everyone focuses on their strengths, output improves across the board.
- Business growth – delegation opens the door to taking on more opportunities without stretching yourself dangerously thin.

- Better work-life balance — having a dependable team allows you to be present where you're needed most.

Delegation is not just a strategy. It's a commitment to building something that doesn't depend entirely on you to survive. And in a business as demanding as auto transport, that commitment is one of the most powerful choices you can make.

KEY LESSONS FROM THIS CHAPTER

- *A failed delegation attempt is not a reason to stop delegating. It's a blueprint for doing it better.*
- *Build your vetting process before you need to use it. Know what your standards are and communicate them clearly.*
- *Letting go of control is not weakness. It's how you build something bigger than yourself.*
- *The right team doesn't just help you do more. It helps you become a better leader.*

CHAPTER 6

Diversifying Income Through Ancillary Services

Building Stability Beyond the Load

Having moved from operating as a motor carrier to providing brokerage services alongside it, I learned something important: versatility isn't just an advantage — it's essential. In a rapidly changing industry where market conditions can shift as quickly as the vehicles we move, relying on a single income source is a vulnerability you can't afford.

Diversification is what transforms a business from something fragile into something resilient.

Broadening your services creates multiple income streams, stabilizes cash flow, and strengthens your business foundation against the inevitable volatility of any single market.

Why Diversification Is Non-Negotiable

For me, diversification was both a business decision and a personal one. As a husband, father, and entrepreneur, I knew that a strong household required a stable financial foundation — and a single income stream in a cyclical industry couldn't provide that consistently.

- Financial Resilience — Multiple income streams protect your business when one temporarily dries up.
- Market Adaptability — Clients increasingly want comprehensive, one-stop solutions.
- Enhanced Reputation — A full-service provider is perceived as more professional and more appealing to clients who want a long-term partner.

Ancillary Services Worth Considering

Vehicle Maintenance and Repair

A natural extension of the auto transport world. Routine maintenance or specialized repair services generate additional revenue while keeping your fleet in excellent condition.

Vehicle Storage

Providing secure, dependable storage addresses a real market need and can be a significant recurring revenue source.

Detailing Services

Offering professional detailing ensures that vehicles don't just arrive – they arrive in exceptional condition. This level of attention elevates customer satisfaction and reinforces your brand's commitment to quality.

Vehicle Transport Brokerage

One year after obtaining our carrier authority, my wife launched a separate brokerage authority. It was one of the smartest moves we made. The brokerage allowed us to bring in additional customers I couldn't personally handle, serve existing clients in regions I wasn't traveling to, and generate revenue without requiring us to be the commercial motor vehicle operators. It created a second business that ran in parallel with the first — with its own income potential and growth trajectory.

Training the Next Generation of Transporters

Diversification, for us, has grown beyond our own operation. We've come to see a significant and growing need in this industry for proficient, professional CDL holders — particularly those who are willing to get the work done with the kind of communication and standards that clients expect.

That recognition led us to position ourselves as consultants. We actively work with people who are exploring the CDL route, helping them understand not just how to get licensed, but how to build a business around it. Especially given the accelerating changes in AI and technology across logistics, the transporters who will thrive are those who understand how to grow vertically — building upward from their core skill set rather than staying limited to a single service or lane.

We train other transporters on how to do exactly that. What started as us figuring out our own business has evolved into a platform for helping others build theirs. And that, to me, is the fullest expression of what diversification can become: not just more income streams, but more impact.

Implementing Ancillary Services: A Strategic Roadmap

Conduct Market Research

Before adding any service, understand the needs of your current and potential clients. What problems are they trying to solve? The answers will guide your decisions.

Allocate Resources Thoughtfully

Assess what you'll need in terms of personnel, equipment, training, and infrastructure. Much of the foundational knowledge I used to build our operational infrastructure came from hours spent watching YouTube before spending a single dollar.

Invest in Training

The quality of any service you offer depends on the quality of the people delivering it. Every person on your team makes choices that impact your entire business.

Market Your New Offerings

Use tools like Google Ads, Salesforce, MailChimp, and social media to get the word out. Curiosity builds relationships — ask other transporters questions. Many need services that would complement their businesses, but haven't yet been exposed to the right solutions.

Navigating the Challenges of Diversification

Find the Right Balance

A friend once came to me excited about entering auto transport, but quickly started piling on service ideas that had little to do with vehicles. When I asked what market demand those services were addressing, he had no clear answer. Spreading yourself too thin with too many unrelated offerings leads to underperformance. Focus on your niche. Grow your offerings from the core of that niche outward.

Maintain Quality Across Every Offering

I still get calls from customers I served years ago because I met their needs with care and clear communication. That same standard should follow you into every new service you add.

Watch the Financials Closely

We once advertised auto detailing on our website until an ad audit revealed it wasn't generating meaningful profit. We removed it. The result? A cleaner, more focused website and better positioning for the services that actually move the needle. Diversification should add positively to your bottom line — not create noise that distracts from your core focus.

The Future of Ancillary Services

- Sustainable Services — As the industry moves toward environmental responsibility, mobile and on-demand services will carry increasing value.
- Technological Integration — Advanced tracking, digital vehicle inspection, and automated customer communication are reshaping what's possible.
- Training and Consulting — As AI and automation reshape back-office functions, the human expertise required to navigate the industry well — and to teach others how to do it — becomes more valuable, not less.

KEY LESSONS FROM THIS CHAPTER

- *Diversification isn't just about income streams. It's about impact. The further you grow, the more people you can bring with you.*
- *Grow your offerings from the core of your niche outward — not in every direction at once.*
- *Measure what you offer. If it's not contributing to your bottom line or your reputation, remove it.*

- *The need for qualified, professional transporters is growing. Position yourself to meet that need — and to train others who can too.*

CHAPTER 7

Streamlining Success

Back Office, Processes, and Systems That Keep You Moving

Early on, I learned something important: behind every successful auto transporter is a strong back office. It's the unseen engine that keeps everything running smoothly. It's where the work is organized, compliance is maintained, and the business is actually managed.

On the road, I'm the face of the operation. But the back office? That's where the real magic happens. It's the starting point of every transport journey, carefully orchestrated to ensure precision, compliance, and consistent execution.

And I'll say this honestly: in this industry, the back office is not just support — it's the heartbeat of the operation. Ignore it, and the business will eventually show the cracks.

The Significance of a Strong Back Office

I've faced unexpected challenges on the road and had to manage them with limited resources. Those moments taught me two things: the value of preparation, and the importance of trusting others to manage what I can't.

Just as a great coach steps back from the court to see the game more clearly, a transporter must build systems that allow the business to operate efficiently — even when they're not behind the wheel.

Core Back-Office Functions

Job Order Processing

Every load begins in the back office. Receiving, processing, and tracking orders — coordinating with clients, managing schedules, and keeping all documentation accurate — this function is the foundation of smooth operations. Roles typically include dispatchers, brokers, mechanical technicians, accountants, and business strategists.

Financial Management

From invoicing clients to managing expenses, handling accounts receivable, and running payroll, the back office keeps the money organized. A financially healthy business doesn't happen by accident — it's built through consistent financial oversight.

Regulatory Compliance

Staying compliant with industry regulations is non-negotiable. Smaller businesses often partner with third-party compliance companies like JJ Keller and Simplex, which provide regular compliance reviews. These include managing licenses, insurance, and registrations, as well as

FMCSA programs like the clearinghouse and human trafficking prevention initiatives. Compliance protects the public — and it protects your operating authority.

Leveraging Technology for Back-Office Efficiency

Process Optimization

Identifying bottlenecks, adopting best practices, and continuously improving your workflows keep your back office running as a support engine, not a drag on operations.

Standard Operating Procedures (SOPs)

SOPs create consistency, reduce errors, and provide a training framework for new team members. If a process matters enough to do regularly, it's worth documenting.

Continuous Improvement

Regularly reviewing and refining your processes is how you stay ahead. The back office should get more efficient over time, not stay stuck in the same habits year after year.

Training and Development

Investing in your team's skills and knowledge is one of the highest-return investments in this business. Companies like JJ Keller and Simplex offer tutorials that train you and your staff in easy-to-understand formats. When employees feel invested in and given opportunities to grow, they perform better — and stay longer.

Building a Collaborative Back-Office Culture

- Hold regular team meetings to encourage open dialogue, idea-sharing, and collective problem-solving.
- Recognize and reward the contributions of your back-office staff. People who feel valued deliver better work.

The Future of Back-Office Operations

- Artificial Intelligence and Automation will continue to simplify routine processes and reduce the need for manual intervention.
- Data Analytics will provide deeper operational insights, enabling smarter

decisions and identifying new growth opportunities.

What's reassuring about managing back-office work is this: it doesn't have to be a full-time obligation. It requires total focus when you're doing it — but it offers genuine flexibility. I've seen experienced drivers successfully transition into back-office management and thrive. The skills translate. The discipline carries over.

KEY LESSONS FROM THIS CHAPTER

- *The back office is not the background. It's the foundation. Treat it accordingly.*
- *Document your processes. Consistency is built on clarity.*
- *Technology should be working for your back office, not the other way around.*
- *The business that runs without you constantly managing it is the business worth building.*

CHAPTER 8

Tools of the Trade

What Every Professional Transporter Needs to Succeed

The greatest influence on my work ethic came from my stepdad — a hands-on man who didn't talk about success so much as he lived it through his actions. He worked tirelessly, built his life from the ground up, and took care of his family without ever seeking recognition for it. For my mother, he provided security. For me, he gave a sense of identity — and a clear picture of what real responsibility looks like.

He operated a car service long before ride-sharing was a concept, fixing and flipping vehicles on the side. He had a gift for spotting potential – finding cars that just needed a little attention and turning them into reliable transportation. I tagged along to auctions, dealerships, and repair shops. I learned how to read a car — not just its condition, but its story. He taught me that every vehicle has a journey and every driver has a purpose.

That early exposure became the blueprint for how I approach my work today. In this business, success isn't just about the miles you log — it's about how well you prepare. The right mindset, the right equipment, and the right systems are what separate a transporter who merely survives from one who truly thrives.

The Transporter's Toolbox: Core Equipment

- Heavy-Duty Tie-Down Straps and Chains — Non-negotiable. High-quality straps and chains keep vehicles securely fastened, protecting the cargo and everyone on the road.

- Winches and Ramps — Essential when handling non-operational vehicles. Dependable winches and ramps can make or break a job.
- Wheel Chocks and Safety Cones — Simple, critical, and often overlooked. They prevent vehicles from shifting during loading and unloading and improve on-site safety significantly.
- Battery Jump Pack, Jumper Cables, Lockout Kit, and Fuel Canister — Cars that sit for extended periods lose battery charge and may not start on their own. A compact portable jump pack handles this without the hassle of traditional chargers. A lockout kit covers you when vehicle doors lock unexpectedly — which happens more often than you'd think, especially at auction or repo yards. A small fuel canister covers vehicles that arrive too low to load or unload safely.

On-The-Road Maintenance Kit

- Basic Mechanic Tools — Wrenches, screwdrivers, pliers, and electrical wiring repair kits are your first line of defense against minor issues.

- Spare Parts — Spare filters, belts, hoses, and bulbs have saved more trips than I can count.
- Emergency Repair Kits — Tire and electrical repair kits belong in every transport vehicle.

Technology Tools That Matter

- GPS Navigation Systems — Designed specifically for trucks, these systems aid in route planning and help you avoid low-clearance bridges and restricted roads.
- Dash Cams — Provide a documented record of road incidents and are invaluable for resolving disputes or insurance claims.
- Electronic Logging Devices (ELDs) — Required for hours-of-service compliance. ELDs help track and report driving hours accurately and efficiently.

Safety Gear

- High-Visibility Safety Apparel — Being seen during loading, unloading, and roadside situations is critical.

- Hard Hats and Safety Glasses — Required protection during certain operations.
- First Aid Kit — A comprehensive kit for minor injuries or emergencies on the road.

Communication Tools

- CB Radio — Essential for communicating with other drivers and staying aware of road conditions ahead.
- Smartphone with Essential Apps — Weather updates, truck stop locators, rest area finders, and load boards — the right apps turn your phone into a mobile command center.
- Portable Wi-Fi Device — Ensures constant connectivity for managing bookings, responding to clients, and accessing critical information on the road.

Comfort and Longevity on Long Hauls

- Ergonomic Seats and Cushions — Reduce fatigue during extended drives.
- Portable Refrigerator and Cooking Appliances — Healthy eating on the road requires preparation.

- Quality Bedding and Privacy Curtains — Rest is not a luxury. It's an operational requirement.

Advanced Tools on the Horizon

- Telematics Systems — Real-time vehicle monitoring and predictive maintenance allow you to address issues before they become costly problems.
- Automated Load Matching Systems — AI-driven platforms that optimize routes and match available loads with nearby carriers are already emerging. Think of the efficiency model Uber uses — that level of automation is coming to auto transport. Stay informed. Stay ready.

KEY LESSONS FROM THIS CHAPTER

- *The right tools are not a luxury. They are the foundation of a professional operation.*
- *Your equipment reflects your standards. Invest accordingly.*
- *Preparation is the most underrated competitive advantage in this industry.*

- *Know your truck the way a surgeon knows their instruments. Your livelihood depends on it.*

CHAPTER 9

Embracing Change and Preparing for the Future

The Road Ahead Is Worth the Ride

I was born and raised in Baltimore City — a place that taught me grit before I even knew the word.

For the first seven years of my life, my world moved by bus and subway. That was our rhythm: waiting at the corner, hopping on the #23, #3, or #8 line, transferring at Charles Street or Greenmount Avenue, and watching the city go by through smudged windows. Those long rides didn't just transport me from one place to another. They taught me patience, endurance, and awareness. I studied people. I noticed expressions. I learned how the city breathed.

On weekends, when we rode in a car, everything changed. The same trip that took two hours by bus took fifteen minutes. My grandparents' old sedan felt like a time machine – smooth, quiet, free. I didn't fully understand it then, but those rides planted something in me. Freedom of movement became a symbol of stability and possibility.

That's where my love for cars began – not from luxury, but from longing. My friends and I used to stand outside and yell, "Myra whip!" every time a nice car passed by. It was our way of dreaming out loud, calling our future into existence before we had the means to reach it. Looking back, I see how those moments trained my mind to visualize abundance even amid scarcity. We didn't have much. But we had imagination – and that was enough to keep us hopeful.

The Things I Said I'd Never Do

I want to tell you something that I think is more useful than any strategy or tip I could offer: a list of the things I was absolutely certain about — that I later learned I was completely wrong about.

Because one of the biggest lessons this journey has taught me is that change doesn't ask for your permission. And the sooner you stop resisting it, the faster you grow.

Here are three things I said I would never do — and now I can't imagine operating without:

I said I needed my own truck to be successful.

For a long time, I believed that owning your equipment was the only real path to credibility and income in this industry. And while ownership has its place, I've come to understand that success in auto transport is far less about what you own and far more about how you operate. There are highly profitable models in this industry built around leveraging other people's equipment, building brokerage relationships, and consulting. The asset matters less than the strategy.

I said I would only do long-haul runs to make real money.

I used to easily turn down local routes. I thought they were too physically demanding and not financially rewarding enough to be worth my time. Then I ran the actual math. Twelve to fifteen local loads over five to six days a week — with less time away from home, lower fuel costs, and more predictable scheduling — could generate solid income and give me something long-haul runs couldn't: consistency and presence with my family.

I found my edge. Knowing your limits and finding your edge is one of the most important things you can do in this business. Some people build profitable operations entirely off the load board. Some build entirely off local relationships. The key is to know which model works for you — not which one sounds most impressive.

I said I didn't need a dispatcher.

I was wrong. A good dispatcher doesn't just find you loads — they protect your time, your income, and your sanity. They build relationships with brokers that take years to develop. They handle the communication that pulls your attention from the road. They see the bigger picture while you're focused on the immediate one.

I was a solo operator for a long time, and I was proud of it. But I've come to see the value of a good team the way I've come to see the value of delegation: it's not about needing help. It's about building something that goes further than you can take it alone.

The Imperative of Adaptability

Over the years in this industry, I've seen how quickly things can change. The auto transport sector is constantly evolving — driven by technology, shifting consumer habits, and new regulations. What worked five years ago may not be sufficient today.

Adapting to change isn't just about survival. It's a growth strategy. Electric vehicles are changing what we transport. Automation is changing how we operate. New logistics technologies are rewriting the rules of efficiency. To remain competitive, transporters need to lean into innovation rather than resist it.

- Embrace Technological Advancements — From GPS tracking to automated load matching, staying current with technology isn't optional.
- Understand Market Shifts — The growth of online car sales has fundamentally changed the traditional dealership model and created new demand patterns.
- Stay Compliant with Evolving Regulations — Emissions standards, safety protocols, and electronic logging requirements continue to change.

A Word on Women in This Industry

I want to say something that I believe with real conviction, and I want to say it clearly: this industry needs more women.

I've observed it firsthand. When my wife speaks with certain clients, the dynamic shifts. The intensity drops. People listen more. They're more open, more receptive, more willing to engage in the kind of conversation that builds a real business relationship. Some of that is her personality. But some of it is something bigger.

Auto transport is, and has been, a male-dominated industry. But what this business actually requires is not dominance. It requires compassion for people. It requires the ability to understand what a client is really asking for, even when they can't quite articulate it. It requires patience, intuition, and emotional intelligence to navigate high-stakes situations without escalating them.

No one does that more naturally than a woman who knows the business.

My wife is able to look at this business from perspectives I simply don't have access to on my own. She has driven. She understands what it means to be on the road, to manage a load, to feel the physical and mental weight of this work. And she understands the back end — the brokerage, the operations, the client relationships. That combination — the dual perspective — is invaluable. It's made us a stronger operation than I could have built alone.

If you're a woman reading this book and considering this industry: the road needs you. Not despite the fact that it's traditionally been a man's world — but precisely because of it. Your perspective, your approach, and your presence will make this industry better.

Diversification as a Long-Term Strategy

Diversifying services and income streams remains central to my business strategy. The transporters who thrive long-term are the ones who build multiple revenue sources, serve multiple markets, and continuously develop their expertise.

Ancillary services like vehicle storage, maintenance, brokerage, and consulting don't replace your core business — they strengthen it. They allow you to serve more of your existing customers' needs and attract new customers who want a comprehensive solution.

Investing in Skills and Knowledge

Continuous learning is not optional in a field that changes as rapidly as this one. The transporters who thrive are the ones who treat professional development as an ongoing commitment, not a one-time event.

Attend industry seminars and conferences when you can. Engage in webinars when you can't. Join online forums and communities where knowledge is shared freely. Turn your drive time into learning time. The investment in your development always comes back to you.

The Road Behind. The Road Ahead.

Looking back, I see how every chapter of my story was preparation for the next one. The Baltimore buses. The incarceration at 17. My stepdad's lessons. The Salt Lake City flight. The pandemic pivot. The Georgia adjustment. Wifey being right. My daughters growing up while I was on the road — and understanding why.

All of it was training.

Resilience isn't about being unbreakable. It's about being rebuildable. It's knowing that when life shifts, you can shift with it — with grace, grit, and gratitude. It's knowing that the things you said you'd never do might be the very things that carry you forward. It's knowing that the person beside you often sees your future before you do.

That's my background. That's my foundation. And that's the spirit behind this book.

The road ahead is yours. Drive it with purpose.

KEY LESSONS FROM THIS CHAPTER

- *The things you're most resistant to changing may be the things most worth changing.*
- *Finding your edge matters more than following someone else's model.*
- *This industry needs more women. If you are one, the road needs you.*
- *Resilience is not about being unbreakable. It's about being rebuildable.*

THE END.

About the Author

Keith Jones is a husband, father, entrepreneur, and licensed auto dealer and broker whose journey is defined by resilience, redemption, and purpose. Born and raised in Baltimore, Maryland, Keith's early years taught him about struggle, survival, and the quiet strength that develops when life doesn't offer easy options.

After leaving school in the 11th grade, a series of poor decisions led to incarceration between the ages of 17 and 20. Yet even within those walls, Keith found something transformative: reflection, accountability, and the power of deliberate choice — values that would go on to shape every chapter of his life.

Upon returning home, Keith began rebuilding from the ground up. He landed a job at Jiffy Lube, where he met the woman who would become his wife and business partner. Determined to overcome the limitations of his past, he launched his first business — an automotive dealership focused on helping underserved communities access reliable transportation and build credit.

Keith and his wife Holli later founded three businesses within the automotive sector, dating back 2019 starting with Eyeconic Logistics, East Coast Auto Broker, and Consultor Plus Auto. Together, they have built a diversified operation that includes motor carrier services, transport brokerage, vehicle sales, and consulting and training for aspiring transporters. They continue to give back through community initiatives that provide school supplies, food, and essential resources to families in need.

Now based in the Atlanta, Georgia area with his wife and daughters, Keith remains anchored in faith, family, and community service. An active member of a local running association, he regularly participates in charity runs — a living reminder that resilience is not defined by where you start, but by how you choose to rise.

Road to Resilience is his first book.

www.ingramcontent.com/pod-product-compliance
Lightning Source LLC
LaVergne TN
LVHW010930110826
845149LV00013B/2537
* 9 7 9 8 9 9 5 1 7 2 6 0 4 *